SONETO UNIVERSAL

ONE
HUNDRED
SOULFUL SONNETS

SONETO UNIVERSAL

PHILIP ISUKAPATI

GYAN

Published by

GYAN

Gyan Publishing House
5, Ansari Road
Daryaganj, New Delhi-110002
Phone: 011-47034999, 9811692060
E-mail: books@gyanbooks.com

Distribution Network
gyanbooks.com
India, USA, Canada, UK, Australia, France

ISBN: 978-93-7169-368-4 (HB)
First Published, 2025

Printed at: Gyan Press, Delhi.

SONETO UNIVERSAL

Author: PHILIP ISUKAPATI

AUTHORED, EDITED AND DESIGNED BY PHILIP ISUKAPATI

DEDICATION

In my deep reflection, I dedicate this literary work to my everloving Brother — Dr. Isaac K. Isukapati.

CONTENTS

Dear reader,

"I write to live or live to write and may live or die but now I write to leave my imprints to the world — is the real cause of my poetic mind."

Words are wonderful, they define everything and the world. This creation or this universe or God in entirety exists through these wonderful words. If words aren't magical or no life, then prayers are null and even God isn't existent. More importantly, the words of the poetic mind travel by oceans and even by clouds, the words of the poetic mind feel the moon or the stars close by, and the words of the poetic mind even feel her illusive love in the skies.

A poetic mind is a cosmic prowess which can hold the entire universe at its will. Blessed are the poets who have those magical words which certainly define you and me, and the entire nature or the universe: the sun, the moon, and the stars as many a time beyond their existence. Poets can think more deeply than what they can as they think to yield very beautiful words the world needs in. Ah! A poetic mind savours thoughts and nothing much pleases it all.

A poet's Retreat

Whispers of the fountain shall lead thy way;
Abound thoughts ablaze to pair with thy
fate:
This fate cajoles thy vanity today;
This way poet's retreat shall reinstate.
Thou art the subtle mind the sun shines;
How trying thy wit changes this tearful world.
Thou leap beyond the universe in rhymes;
"thy chimes" tune to shape us be mimed.
Thou are the great mind which angels share;
The art all that worth which bears thy paint:
The raiment thou bear saintly with thy care;
Her wildly rife here so wildly to taint.
But why do the poets "thou" few agree?
And how do our thoughts a free flow to thee?

The earth of Me

O! Not even the balm will her wounds heal,
And what I think and drink that I shall seek!
But I never sell duck nor devil's seal
Of sands, of lakes or of beacons to bleak.
O, will I thunder to brief how stars dwell?
Showing all to wonder how twinkling hall;
Heydays with this bewitch if I'm to tell,
My loft to benedict that I'm thy call.
Yet come mine — strays my sweetness
I arrive,
And instant sparks in men thou lead much craft:
Like nature and beauty, vigor derive
When from thy help to — there our woods
subvert
Or this Earth of me that I propagate:
My bent is fruit let beauty bloom fate.

Love or Like

What shall make me love a woman to drive?
And how shall I love this woman just like?
Those roses lips which bud a love to thrive,
And how shall I love this woman war like?
When shall I look at her while she ever lists,
And why should I touch her cheeks to my
greed?
Those blushing fears and her love life to wits,
And why should I love her like extreme
speed?
Every day I wake up in her surprise,
But all she hates when I behave love life!
When she wears not my crown in her surmise,
Then why should I love her like the unwise?
This love gratis but "like" shall bliss her more
When "like" rarer than "love" exists in core.

The Ant

When the ants of the east are living for peace,
Having their anthills near a bay — their way;
Not inside the trunk of a tree — their niece,
As huts of mud and clay perished this day.
O, they searched their huts inside New York
towns
And interior hamlets as hillocks frown!
When a crazy gloom razed their living grounds,
We drained mud into our towns with the crown.
How can the pleasure of human leave harm?
Alas! They lost their dream of mud or clay.
When these ants travelled to their frozen
farm,
They all would search for their tree at a bay.
But not even one hut at the near dry
When all their mud and clay dried up their try!

Money or Honey

When she said, “you are my money let’s play,”
But I asked, “are you ready to be my mate?”
Then she said, “you are my honey let’s fey,”
I quipped, “your charm fills my sensuous taste.”
If you call me money or honey — chase,
Then why not choose either its tail or head.
If you pine money to come to thy place,
Why you call me honey while I heard.
Here in the lone spring — I see her to dress:
A long cloak till her feet, pure white in vast.
There I admire her dark exotic eyes;
Along the miles, we walk to talk the best.
But how can money yield my love to thee?
As thou can drink honey without money.

Pearl of Love

Pearl, thy life in pain; thy life had to pay!
Before thou had formed, thou lived in calm.
But a spectral sand which had spread thy
balm;
Thou died in despair since nowhere to way!
Grow, glow my eyes know thy shadow's grace,
O Grace of thine when thy mace shall be lead;
Twist is thine, mist is mine and glow my guise
That twinkle like thy droplet's shine be spread.
Like the pearls of love — thou my strand in verve,
And when I wear, thy touch shares my full life.
The balm which spreads to rejuvenate thy nerve
That thou drive from a speck of sand in rife.
I wear thy shine and it's a shrine in thee,
And wed with pearls which shine my love for thee!

The Tree

Trees in rife — yield life, an honour to say;
They shine in the sun shine, Ah! Fruits
derive.
Pray to the clouds above for the trees to play
In the rains that fall when their calls arrive!
Men of the times, who bask under the shed
Or shades of the tree where they breathe
to gain!
The airy fair is all that air, all glad;
Her branches blow let the cool air way in.
The Moon with no trees but we can't test;
There aren't stars which carry air near.
The bizarre talk is never to the gust,
But placate sighs which no one is aware.
Why do we fell trees in the winter binge?
How one can part a tree; himself "revenge!"

Addiction, He has crowned

Knotting her scarlet "addiction!" he has crowned;
Heartless of her jest corners with his plea.
When words unlocked his spears to set her free —
O! His small mot then, leaves ease to her bond.
A million chimes of her claps did prowl around,
Blithe lits eons swooped elixir in sniff —
His scarlet has sauntered; flown to the cliff.
He bid the actress with her soul mourned:
Her mercenary accrue to astound!
She has sneered at a racer; called him damp;
He has snuggled in the dark — there a swamp.
Dwelling around the spot of Hilton's land,
His sting has come perfect hence, she could brew:
O, his heart warming games so much in dew!

The Jail

Hear not those chirping birds — I'm at the bay,
But a jail a bright mind for me inspite!
Don't call it a curtailed freedom but say:
The will of the mind which calls no respite.
My spirit can raise within the walls or sails
Since, a jail a live hell but my freedom.
A freedom of thought in this hall avails,
O heart! My heart! It's my mind "freedom."
Through a focussed energy of gale,
My mind can mend mine so hard to be tough
That my wandering thoughts in me for sale:
A sale of wisdom while a pun to laugh!
Why do we dodge as if it were a folley?
How could we not know about its jolly?

Femininity

Days should rapt thee when dew of love thou
bend,
Blazing at the bay, thou found a guy;
Thou held him tight but sank in a quicksand:
Help was the cry which thou had shouted high.
At thy own image in mirror — no gain;
Bower by thy side but thy helpless cry.
Pleaded to his twist when mercy was pain
While living in the dark — he had to lie.
Thou tied his poses, etching him in mind,
But his wrath was what thou could only bank.
Thou in a whirl as thou sank in his hand,
He found tears in thee; whirls as thou sank.
But fate didn't leave as thou bear his pain;
Nine months passed, a tender cry bears thy gain!

Prince and the Pretty

Prince and the pretty are friends while we say;
He looks at gritty girls but slows his gait.
O! They wait, long they wait for him to stay;
Mutes his loving tone but all of them wait!
Tried that he tried for no pretty a face,
And their grace like bevy runs fates be read:
His calm, his taste and his fate fill their space
That they flee his fantasy — they should wed!
A tall and slender beauty holds his gaze,
And blazes a fire while she turns tough.
Circles him as her dancing feet in craze,
This woman like a sylph shall smile and
laugh.
But he looks at the one with no joy or glee;
Holds her arms; lifts her in the air to free!

A poison for Me

Your fragrance fills all in my way o- day,
But it's this evening, I'm into your bait;
Your beauty I define and I'm to say,
O thee, my fragrance you stay all my wait.
When I walk along — your memories race,
Which I see in my gait, will you not read?
Low in my car that I'm alone to face;
How I'm forgetting myself in my head.
None ever drives me crazy I may l e,
As my lies are about you in my trough;
I'm in my dreams that you're yet to ply,
As I'm filled with all the weights of your stuff.
How your fragrance pairs outside my duty
Which has become a poison for me!

My love,
A missive

My love, a missive and my dove — passive!
How years of yearning and joy of weeping,
Try days that miss to kiss mine — the pensive:
Wait! A delectable dusk in sans sobbing!
Date which chimes shall come when I run
astray;
Thou miss my laughs, cries and tears of vast.
Lone roses of my gay while I'm astray;
I listen to what parrot says, O! Heart.
A dove to fly while eagle grips her back,
Her feathers torn away, while her tears cry.
O! Missive that thou cry while I shall trek,
I may cringe; inspire a missive to fly.
Fall from above into a gripping hall,
But thou another firmament above all!

Silence in Fate

Above, below is my love so thou bind,
O! This life with so much love which thou
lend.
Care for care, I love to spend so I send
Much needed roses for thou to bend.
Jewels in jewels O, thou come so blind:
Here, I'm not to glimpse thy wealth like a trend.
Close much close thy braces which can endorse
For me to love thy embrace like a rose:
Fragrance its fragrance miles away it shows,
All along my footsteps — thy fragrance grows.
Dark in the night thou wear jasmines to pose:
I come so near, thou shy away to close.
At first I glance then I watch; then I wait,
But thou shut thy door in silence in fate!

Sky, my Love

Thou throw me into the waters as I play,
But my eyes never turned away your wait;
The airy mist has whirled over my way,
But couldn't petrify me, it's your bait.
You poisoned air — my many lone days,
And you turn fears of my tears in red;
I face agony but offer prayers,
And my ways find your deep hate in my blood;
Whirls in the wind whisper at me and lie,
But I shrugged my shoulders at ears deaf;
There live silences for a longing tie —
Braces in eternity which I buy:
Your love in its fragrance, a love-fortune;
You say, "sky is my love; why am I late?"

Strife

Softness in sunrise blink upon my day;
Remorseless bowers hide worldly desires free.
Chirping until night — birds in quest
embrace me,
While helpless a soul calls her in my way.
Does rain feign what be mine which she deflected?
“can fights hide” a breeze like love — I’m adroit!
Seal my living boredom non detailed hence rest;
Glue myself in thine should herself dejected.
Roseate her lustre — has to choose a frock;
Wish me be her side, a fanciful gl de.
I glow over her face while ride her pride
When my kisses and her abode be my freak.
It’s how my little fight; my love for thee,
But how can I blink that shine before thee?

Feign

Flow or glow is thy love touching wind;
Thy eyes so bright, I might not whisk or fend.
My art depicts thy beauty — plenitude,
But thou fly so far in vicissitude.
Thy dream from my near, runs deep in the
sky,
But I'm here in lassitude, I can't fly
For which I cry in the winds and the sun,
But thou laugh afar and look back to pun.
I look up at the sky only to sigh,
But my breath I kept and my life not die.
This life and thy life thou carry in clouds;
Thou fly too high while I fall in thy love.
O, feign there be none to carry me safe —
I fall and I fall so deep from the clouds!

Magical Woman

Quirky quintessence be bridal choir
While plenty of roses wait for her to wear.
I breathe her poise at a nearby fire,
And fly to her like a seagull in flair.
She appears unsure yet she is calm
While I travel miles for peace in my town.
When I sleep deeply, triggers an alarm;
In sensuous pose, she comes in her dawn.
Keeping the curtains far behind my chill,
I touch beloved cheeks at the near downhill.
Her lovely feel on the chariot's wheel,
Between me and her while a deepened deal.
Winds be so calm when hills bending to face,
But this magic woman: my tears to grace!

Pain

Deep inside my heart “pain” I ever feel,
And a recall to the streams where I live;
Thy voices I hear right in my zeal,
Stifling mourn to overcome fear and live;
Losing thy pair while I run down my tears,
And they form a river which flows thy near;
I run on my feet but fall in layers,
But love relentless forms sentinel spear;
Lo! Thy grace of what an amazing mace,
Like a witchess — thou touch me with thy
wand;
Thou capture mine soul but disown my space
While my lasting streams run after thy bond;
How far thy wand in den, a shielded ken?
O heart! I search while uncover my pen.

Plenty Cry

My mistress why bear if I've to spurn?
But murals be more glad when her lips speed.
If toes be knights O, men's lure waits for none;
She be a fire when witches swear her dread.
How could she be a mire or leeche's
mud-wed-strait?
Yet, how seas glee when she can't ever speak?
But her fumes do live any more twilight?
I will breathe to let in this actress speak,
But her eagle like nature sneaks; kills her foe,
And her tragic loathe adores musings around.
I chant — whoever chants the actress Joe:
She — my mistress talks and hates on the
ground.
Let me enliven O, my new affair,
Plenty there cry but firewalls appear.

No Faith

I ever touch her cheeks to start my day
While her eyes smile to wide open her date.
Her bliss above and the sky below — force play;
Thoughts survive only on a perfect slate.
Her beauty undo her jacket in grace,
And her curly hair covers her bust — void.
Devouring curves of the world what she shares;
Phoenix passes above her verse to plead.
I bid her love throne — which has all my grain,
But she lifts hers arms to embrace her past.
That her spark flouts my passion in her pain
While her memory fades away so fast.
Why did she leave her memory to flee?
That she can disgrace very faith in me.

Choose her Fear

I look at her wings in a pensive whim;
Look at her scar and painted span of grim.

Lo, she trudges a lonesome dusk and wins,
But on her skin, I have pierced my prints.
I hook her when she has pale milcly lips
While she's leaving her skin to the wings.
When her chatters mild like a bliss to croon;
She's lovely in her mild-bright-golden
room.
When roseate lips sing — a fairy moon,
Her blossom shines amidst my dry days soon.
Go to pretty cheer; go to her near:
Her bosom tells mine to choose her fear.
My closed eyes, choose her fear from so near,
O, her estranged winds — no longer here.

Paint my Heart

A paint of my heart wore a lonesome ray
When depth of my touch ran deep in
her hair;
Marvel hues died at the fate of my day
When blistering summer moved in her air.
Tidings, dexterity or purity:
A cherub so shied as heydays so vied;
A wintry surmise with prosperity:
Angelina! My feet found a way so wide;
My touch of thy hide like touching thy tide
Added mirth of thy thoughts like a toy;
True kisses of thy heart O! My heart's guide,
Angelina: a real joy, cloy or ploy.
But Angelina's beauteous panache,
Until kisses print her eyes like a collage!

Freedom

When my wings fly for thee above the sky,
There I fall to the ground in a wink;
My freedom! My freedom! That when I fly,
My wings broken for which let my grounds blink;
A running feet to the runnel espy
For my limbs broken but my peaceful stay;
My freedom! My freedom! That when I fly,
Like a pegasus above skies today;
A cry, I hear at the far away plot,
And I hear all at the far away ground;
Joy! A joy, I hear from far away knot,
But my heart freed to fly her from the bond!
Into my lonely mind, thou shall exhort,
O! Mystic, a freedom of these wing's heart!

Love Life

This morning shine which may rhyme my
soul's goal;
Her love for roses red — a twinkling prowl.
Up the hill — kisses stray lone in my dole;
Wild stemmed flowers — a melancholy's soul.
O soul, she twirls her harness till this day
While in the dark, she holds my breath in lead.
Time and date "candlelight shrine" life at gay,
Deaf-true-self; blind ourselves — all pun
till bed.
Cuddling wildly romance of distinct blood
From the pure love of his truth, he shall share.
On the roses bed and when she shall spread:
Trails or cherished moments ebb or dare!
How her aura when my soul savors mourn,
But — that song will prolong in ever thorn!

A hunger Cry

I enter into thy world — thy freedom,
But search my freedom is my call's "motiff."
Thy grace upon my face but like a tomb;
Vigor thou demonstrate but my life tough!
Rejoice is thy name for thy hell's nature;
The satan behind never let me face —
But taunts with a life's puzzling curvature:
The checkered evil, he checks at my pace.
Hate — awaits, I'm not late but it's a bait,
Yes, it's a human trap that my rights died.
Beneath the stars O, this darkness to wait
For the souls of the world that I'm to hide.
What if I go to weep, why don't they care?
Yes, the real power above may dare!

Nature

Lovely rainbow finds the sky on her way,
And the dusk of the winds flow her favorite.
There pairs a chearful fragrance on my way,
But beautiful fair of eyes, the world to
pyrate.
Her morn in my mourn shall have wings;
Her sundry moods which fill my abode.
A gem which she wears has her pals,
Calling my hope of destiny to breed.
Nature's fragrances of rime to enflame,
But how this fragile nature — no not let.
Those brawny citadels which we all care,
Have filled murmurs of our narure's fret.
Joy, thou fugitive but gave nature to me:
A thousand poses which I care to see!

The world of Arms

When I turn my soul to thee, my soul's cry;
What I seek to thee — the world may bereave!
I speak my words to thee then heart will try,
And thy feed may reach for spirits alive!
The bold who weds then his blood be his
shed
When wildness turns cruel against his grain.
Dare is the pain and witches find the dead
For much acuity prevails amidst rain.
Churning deeds veil a dream, it's no crusade
That they cry and cry or drink noxious Earth.
If this world fraught with dire arms to
parade
That well we shall inflict for conspired death!
O, how do we raise arms for our living?
And why do we need arms for our dying?

Love,
a Paradise

When hills and dales sowed thy beautiful flair,
Those flowers profuse had scented her tale;
I stood by her side with my gentle stare,
And blew my dare upon an awesome gale;
I asked her hand — be my side in my sail,
And I pledged to her smart cavalier air;
As her bosom friend, I stood on life's nail,
And flew my wings for a sprighted affair;
Heaven in my sighs: my ravishing hale,
Her countenance flames, her silhouettes's shade;
Gritty her image but my pensive veil,
Virgin of the woods, a nuptial bride;
Should she ever hear my love life reprise?
A constellation honored paradise!

Heavenly Grace

Loved by purity and by honey blend,
She has churned to bear his sport; grown his bliss.
He has gripped her in surprise "balance veiled,"
Which brought her so many of his love shades.
Love, art and growth had called him to her game;
She would embrace him in a graceful dare.
What a mystical name her guiled fame
When nature graced him in her frantic flair.
How her mystical win over his talk?
That was the prank which her beloved laughed!
Said her heart, only cheer or love but dark;
Lo! Her heart, his heart be with cheers amassed.
Now, he feels neither her voice nor face;
He looks at her space in heavenly grace!

Love tears Or smiles

Now that I love her, I hug my love brace:
Know not her depth of love, as I must wait.
Her soul can teach mine — leaving to a fight,
But the end or beginning has her ways.
I ever know how to love her always,
And know to lead her by my hug so tight.
Love like life immense with her; I strive bright,
Mine! A love-true-life as I dream to raise.
I fill her with pouring love mine — infuse
That wriggling love like a deep floral breath.
Life filled glitters be found but I may lose,
As every step of mine, leading to dearth!
Love tears or smiles, know now that I choose —
But she is no near mine but choose wealth!

Heart Cried

Where in the skies that I shall dwell to be?
And why will my darkness just fade away?
But what if the twinkle lit up my glee,
And here on my dimple thy droplets sway!
Why ever hover in the night's astray?
And ever you embrace my wit in trail.
Wow, how the stars shone in the lonely day,
But why thou muted to shy to leave my wail?
What if my glimpses which loved — stared for thee;
How could there be winds as thou standing still.
Why shuddering heart touched in the night's free?
But that surreal bliss lo! You hid to shrill.
Why in the night explored my beloved but died?
All that I loved why my heart said while cried!

Love her Dream

Wondrous, bosoming; never failing love:
Flowing cupidity glows loving vow.
O love, tell times that I'm thy pride so true;
Keep promises in the pride like my hue.
Set thy shine while cues of mine can be true
When these happy hours are set to allure.
This east behind and her faith pure virgin,
And such truly love I shall never grin.
The picture I drew for her is my brink
When my words describe her flaring cheeks
link.
O, those memories fondle her to think,
But my eyes glow to show her not to blink.
I buy her love fragrance to love her sheen,
But her sublime fame, a love dwindling dream.

A true Shrine

A pouring rain yet my soul's gentle flame;
The lonely date where she can be my pal.
Thrill enslaves my love for her very name,
And this fairy tale which my soul won't null.
My ever doting love, a humming morn:
Leads the grace her’s, rebounding in the air.
That her cheeky lips, lusty feel alone
When beauty be bare or rarity there.
And these summer flowers by the Sunset,
For a thousand bird's chirping to engross.
Dutiful I'm but thy beauty has left,
Mine in despair but still holding this cross
That the hope holds the lamp of love mine,
Flames near to enshrine; dine for a true shine!

Chatters live to Die

Near a beautiful stream when my heart
speaks
Of this music's fall, a radiant gall.
I'm wandering between autumn and creeks
When a dearly chill basks to recall.
Love song of thy heart at perilous low
While echoed in the ears of the dark.
I'm at the corner — thou stride miles above,
We cross more caverns while sailing we balk.
This darkness steals in the strides of our stay
When the sunset calls for the dusky dew.
Shielding thy way but meadows hug my gay
To live to die, pleasure hallowed thy hue.
My acquaintances impregnate thy song,
O charm! O love! Insurmountably strong!

Raindrops or Tears

My distress away be fun with raindrops
That delight by her nearness — I am wet:
Hope or bliss or joy which she never stops
When I'm close to my boredom, she should set!
My mistress gushes, I run at the sea
Where we stand alone on her raindrop bed.
Her erstwhile where I find her joy to see
There I shall play or frisk or risk on bed.
My embrace hugs her on clouds may long live,
And more her pleasure which weathers so vast.
A play that I play like her toy — may give:
All my joy which I enjoy raindrop frost!
She stands in the winds which yields her tears;
But I choose her tears — not raindrop showers.

Fowl Play

Giggles in the dark at the weird dust;
A shadow of the beast — a circled grin!
Here were the deeds of the darkest to win,
As this queen yielded herself in their lust.
A living queen but for the heaven's sake;
They found her somewhere in her blissful
themes!
Lo, they were the marauders of the crimes
As their joy dinned at the west of the lake
Hence, their elements circled her in ache
While they ran down to her foothill to sin.
There was no solace to her blinking chin,
As their joy sucked her at this Vampire's lake.
O, she lived in the deep dark for their gay;
They played with her life each and every day.

Hold her Faith

When I enkindle her countenance in grace
I hold her bosom in her freedom's faith;
Her road to tour braces the tempest mace,
But leaves a lip to like a sleeping swathe;
I'm yearning to breathe her fire in my trail,
O! Her flame of torch, a great glory to craze;
Across the vale — I marched in a frail,
Frisson and hail but my caged passion's rage;
Upon these gusty winds — flowers to miss
Over the ocean's sail to surpass her muse;
Her addiction — my defeat but I drink its bliss
In the fierce girl's kiss while blushing ruse;
She painted my face in a rosy guise
In the warmth of love's eternal capsize.

So far in Me

A million years past, love mine carves a way;
My heart's overflow when she's by my gait.
Chattering winds in her gentle touch stay,
Close to my heart so heavy that I wait.
Rave of pleasure at her rhyming dance
When her romancing stance of my eyes lead.
Those doves show a way so, her way
I glance —
And here is her play whence I rest my need.
Wide open eyes fill her charm, can't I buy?
My soul deeper in her love to engulf.
But she comes now, down to mine in a sly;
Much of her disguise — beauty in her laugh.
But why doesn't she try what love may plea?
And how will she sleep so much far in me?

The Satyr

Where in the dark the licentious satyr lived;
While in the wild, angel's pure attire — grave.
What if the demon's evil razed her naive,
And the esprit shed her spirit's veil — lied.
Her moaning winds wried in glee of that night,
And there the stalker prodded her in shame.
Cues of the wild where a bewildered fight;
The might to a more desperate blood game.
There the Angels met her; shied her bangles
And left to heaven while pride to their grin.
There the blood of winds had refreshed Angels,
No! Unnerved the men who dressed satyr to sin.
But why was the world blame her to condemn?
And why did the angels sick to her clan!

Now I wonder

Now I wonder how my life has a way,
Here I laugh in this stark world at a bait,
And what her silence which is a oath today
Dodges with mine aimless, through my soul's gait.
To dart therefore "my lover" her presence,
Why lure her heart's bent that her love so wide.
When her path lacks track, my fight is tiring,
But I warmly seek and patience is essence.
Her whispers as replies, her soul in cry —
The man I'm her own drift; why is she tough?
Bear her mind awake can lead her to tie
My princely state, a thousand roses laugh!
And lover her and night skies lovingly:
She swerves close to mine heart with caringly.

Bliss Dives

Hell's sigh vampire's flight threw her lust in sway...
O, flirt more heavenly had worn desperate!
Tough trends woke the curling hugs of a bay;
Sent glimmering breeze brought her to glue date.
I dined and rued the sight for seven times;
Her blend might soften my whole diction
trimmed.
Teary mire would dare in all proclaims,
And dance or gestures sang words merely sinned.
But her ethereal shimmer should not evade,
Her pose perfection of; yet her glare lowest
Nor well breath hug how simplest be her trade
What sublime shone her fame that she sowest.
Prolong! When sin could wreathe and wise could see,
How song tried when bliss dived, leaving at sea?

Bold Heart

Sorrow spurted on her face and her wail;
Lovely roses crushed her name what a shame!
Of her breast or lust or trust — she could fail,
But how would she face his natural game?
How in her win she had sinned while he hymned?
But her drudge bearded at her own smudge.
That she had struggled, trudged or atleast calmed,
But how will she reckon her strife so large?
Of the human surge but her door steps closed;
Noise or choice or verity said:
Her muses, poses or things exposed
Of tosses or lapses or losses — knell.
How deep was her sorrow which he sinned?
So bold was her cold heart while throbbed or winced!

The Monk

If by the constraint should hearts ever think
Then like an austere, a man's practice.
He lives to breathe while minimal to drink,
And his reverence — nature achieves!
He wears mask — no decimation to life,
And a vegan, leaves no pain to the Earth.
Doesn't wear sandals for a micro life
So he fits his naked feet; achieves worth.
Of others unconstrained life fraught with vast;
Their thoughts so pervasive to sprawl like the mud
That they outshine the life of a monk in taste,
But the burden they impose here to lead
For those uncountable lives to flee
O! Those decimated trees they've cut free!

Bleak Pot

When she threw mine soul into a bleak pot,
Those florid wrappings resembled a wild haste.
I tied to the clock at the Sun shine and
sought —
But blithe woes in my sail to fell apart.
When can be fawn indeed guide her in love?
But her vicious bends — a heartless night.
She had frozen doves within a placid floe
That mammoth offense, borne a tarnished sight.
How could aggrieved sever to the bygone?
But chivalry from crow to dove — clever.
Ha! Sad mount of lore that a sermoned moon,
Ditched her play but life wouldn't dare so far.
But stiffened the tail by link, glued to mend:
My aces were best sowed to narrow her bend.

Heart's Clutch

Thy grace I shall not fade away from thee
For thy shackles turned into anklets — rhyme:
Thy freedom be my grace along thy clime,
And all that dust disappear from me.
Where will I find so exquisite visage?
And how can I dare at thy bosom's wild?
Never can my heartthrob says — it's so mild,
And now, thy wish — so fulfilled in my gaze.
Lo, where in the wild winds thy lust should hide?
But what if my deep gaze that can beguile.
What if my heartbreak when thy bust tied
Then, truth and love together be docile.
But why did thy beauty clutches my way?
And when I die deeper into thy way!

Tie her Grace

Strumming mildest chords in his affair's gaze,
And staring her deity's pose can lit his kiss.
His hypnotic transfix carries her breeze,
And lanters so bright might tell her his wish.
Her hurt flares at him is so light — belies,
And their shame lits a sensual duel.
Mocking the divine; her ascendance tries:
Herself his foe when street itself "cruel."
So much low, this bold princess argument;
How her emerald shines — a gawdy ring!
But her spinning feet grounds over his bent,
And a musket hurled — tender date's longing;
Gritty the bold and bless her spartan — he
To pleat a gold hue and tie and grace him.

Die before You leave

Are there whispers in my ears but far away?
Will her vesper while she strands too late?
Born to cheer and her smile to greet my day;
How my laughing soul will know her update.
Winds of truth while those folks move like a race,
Fleeting from the sun for pun but so hard,
Every little brittle settle to face
O, late in the Moon, I've found her bed.
She shirks my fate, but I'm close to her why?
Between the hills — love so fresh that I puff!
Sleeping in the wild with no one, she'll cry;
I reach her behind, make her calm — let's laugh!
She turns my side, looks so deep as her plea,
"I shall die before you leave — wait for me!"

Surreal Dove

Surreal dove! When shall I turn to thee?
As thou shall shower beauteous above.
My sureal dove like the Moon I feel thee,
As I turn to thee to thy love to sow.
My soul while in another heaven to croon;
Thy tunes at the creek — be sold in a trade.
Thou bespeak this truth in my heaven's boon,
As thy songs pervade while the years fade.
Like a morning bliss, thou my purest frost;
My eyes — still remind my serene isle's cruise.
Thy vigor is strong yet thy love so soft
Like a lasting fragrance of princess muse;
Save promises in old antics to glow
While thou give me an old wine to sip love.

The will to Drink

Spying your naive, how should I cue or chant?
Love in a bower tests chimes of desire!
Then lonely tunes crush time O, occult
bent
For voices brood which I shall enquire.
Just a blink, your golden thoughts of power:
Theist I'm but lies govern — deadlock for you.
Ink your links — sweetness in your dense bower
While men be hive to wed the honey dew.
Why do resolve bewitch perilous fall?
When her way finds in me for her firegrass
That lakeside bereaves to vent brink of fall,
But I rave: sleepy bower, shower and rose.
Woo her a booze that is how my love will;
Lead many strings, there she drinks at my will!

We
can be Free

Flow thy turn in my way — my honey day,
And the raindrops which I taste, be my gait.
Thy clutch and my clasp that's all I should say,
And I need thy life — lend me thy raiment.
Showers of rain fall in the loving brace,
And thy shimmers dance which ram me
instead.
I douse in the fun to sin but thy race;
Far in the sky, a sparkle when I head.
No one in mind but a haven — I lie,
That I wait for thee at Chapel Hill's cliff.
Moor my love, I shall moor thy toe; thou sigh:
Whisking those moments while no one be tough!
Why are we late when what we know we see;
Our future shall be bright: we can be free!

Breakup

Shall I keep thee in my eyes any way?
For that I'm into the threads of thy bait.
Which thy love my side will take me today,
O, this life of mine born in for thy sight!
When shall I run and run for love of thy
grace?
Thou take a chance which lures me to thy
bed.
How shall I run at thy pace or thy brace?
I can't fly or go from my love so I wed.
Why I humble in thee, my heart shall
lie;
Thou will not abide when I bend but tough.
Thou may not heed while find mine as a cry;
I say — I'm not proud but bow while I brief.
Oh, thou ran and very much so lonely
That thou couldn't look back at all at me!

Love and Play

Under the Moon — she would be a great
prey,
Why avoid If ever catch her to date.
I held her arms but her fall at the bay;
There she be lewd till too late, it's her fate.
She showed me freedom with her love
ingress;
Should I not thunder when she be naked?
O, wonder mine and her love paradise
If she would ever fall her heart in bed.
And what if I blink but frisk at her sigh?
I must stand by her side at her trough.
Of trance's or man's chances or her try
While she frisks or runs deep into her
rough.
She may fall and cry but most unlikely:
I will hold let she be told that I'll be!

Inside her Scream

I heard my behind at these touching hills
That I heard a scream of an untold dream.
Thoughts of that scream which ran down
to the rills
To search my behind and her far end whim.
Her behind, Ah! She died for her beloved;
Along the rivers — her shadow had left shame.
But the crescent moon and her scents
hallowed,
A decade of her past while seen in fame.
She walked her gait like a romantic teen,
But a night darker which she further screamed!
She leaned, Ah! Screamed her dream across his
sheen,
Yet her soul vanished in the dark had weaned.
She was bugged in her fate and so she died,
But she had left her scream which her dream
surmised.

Lonesome Winds

When shall I fly to heaven to kiss thee?
Or dive to the nadir and search my ken.
Thou art the lovely roses filled in me,
But rough waves to pass by frail — my den!
When the wilder winds leave in a shorter time,
This winter mist veils in a misty maze.
I am to the queen for the times to rhyme,
But her golden wings flinch near a blaze.
Thou every fairy to fly by my side,
But her missing hues shall fill all her sail.
If this eternal love shall not abide,
My sail to eternity shall all fail.
She lives alone inside my lonesome winds
For long live thee inside my trembling strings!

Her Love

Hearts have less meaning to pair than to love;
When will she wear floral trance which could
swear,
A flight so higher in her splendid flow.
This heart now oaths her touching care;
The purity of her feel: love and lust
Shine in her; I may stare her love and try.
Open to the seas and I'm to the dust
When love glints or flies in the selfless high.
Never did she more fascinating roses fill
Than her misty eyes, lips, curves embed;
Never did I see her beauty so chill
While the birds warble at her sweetness shred,
Lovely love! O, my true love blooms at thee,
Yet my mighty heart is waiting, still plea!

Love
Lip

When shall I be searching for my lover?
Garlands in threads of mine, she needs a fan
Of her fragrant dater: love, truth, and pen.
Tie her love stealth of gall and flower:
Brave fit her reticent girlish power
Of forward hoppiness, her fetish stern;
Her love on my lip; turns to me to sin.
Her behive which dances: love, life hover!
My goal does strike a scar, O occult start;
I have a choice gone around, as free:
Her walk to caverns, a celest which flee
While is a wonder on a full moon start!
In blissful loveliness, I bet my day:
The holy deity of herself leads to fey.

Chimes which Rhyme

How her beautiful cheeks so calm and smart
O, her pure love is like a mountain dew.
Limitless in love is her tender heart:
He bubbles with her love so pure to woo.
Like a mantle volcano over the sea,
His anger has frozen at her belief
Whence her perpetual love sings to plea,
And stands like a miraculous relief.
My love, thou walk until the far till end;
My faith, thou walk until reaching its steep.
Where Arabian glee in pearls may blend —
Show how Serbian sea hushes her lip.
Her gossips be the hearts wonderful chimes,
O! My heart beats faster all that she rhymes.

Tears wet & Tears met

Way to the reason now; a doleful dove
Where is my wisdom to plow; tender love.
The gripping soul is the love; I'm so close
In the sands of time for her touching pose.
Bewitching sunset — a play in my dole;
Here is the trip to an atoll — her goal.
The splendour enthralling is all her soul
In the sparkling moonlight, I find a fowl.
The ripples in her heart hides tears now,
And it's that waiting time goes past her bow.
But her hand in mine leads her pregnant woe;
The streams at the palms which flow music
slow.
Tears wet and tears met — all we know;
A soulful thrill or wishful drill: I bow.

The first Night

The summer, a slumber when I'm at bay,
Whether I pray or die, my love a bait.
The number in mind for which I'm at gay;
How I can move or wait, her stance whence late.
Her sprinking bliss or kiss is heaven's grace,
But her cries fall on my shoulders instead.
Her frisking feet of youth at devil's pace
When her hips move her skirt — heartbeat's speed.
Her heartful smile in the winter shield dares
To untie knots, turning her naked feast.
She feels abashed in this winter but stares;
Her beautiful curves uncovered in twist:
My naked faith flowing wild which I see;
Her tears fall on my shoulders in glee!

Words of Love

Where are those words thine which chase me
today?
But here is thy strong thread which knits our
date.
Thou hear in the dark which my heart shall
stray
For thee I am, even when heavens be late.
The spright of life is the life of thy mace,
And thy lonesome ways to cuddle me wed.
When the wounds shall filleth our love to race,
My darling love sings the best of the bed.
When the truth prevails, let me be thy trust;
Thou be my thrill, joy and sorrow and laugh:
Living for eternity at the crest
Whence thy words run deep like sweet sounding
graph.
The strength of thy words; life which loves me,
Allow me love thee for me to set free.

Love Letter

Her sparkling eyes bright and flowers a way;
Her beauty in skinny tights: she is great!
Amazing looks she has: cheer me today;
My joyful thoughts fit her embrace to date.
Shadows shall spin her footsteps in my dreams,
All that she dances in a movements spread:
Her grace whence my sin has love — which she wins;
I walk behind her mind when her words said!
There she can find her ways to fall in place,
And for me to meet her — what should I bet?
As her perfume like poison kills days,
Idyllic hasty past prolong my debt.
How I get her permanent love for me;
Why she should share her love so true to me!

Love Song

Why can't I glee her twinkle in my glow,
But admire guise of the night while jinx springs.
Haughty with the girl that I do not know,
But fresh her soft plump that sows my musings.
O, my agony sip upon her sheen;
Her soft bolden stand let it be trend first.
Chanting thy psalms, fetches her rhyme to feast;
Said my perusal, "she shall want me clean."
I take a sniff in a long breathing air;
Chancing the wand above — her jolting hair
That's how my grit which impacts her hair:
No "cross" to save that night from her despair.
Why this love much — teen hangs on to chat
With fire over her head — mostly to wed.

A midnight Sham

Gorges have depths so deep and fear shall
bear —
Fantacies run waste but lanterns amuse.
Dares at her hell but happy chances to swear;
Wings grow her around and trees love her
muse:
Birds sing great while her beauty speaks duty;
How best I beget to love her instead?
My worth may cease, but I grow my deity;
Harness is the mirth while my dream be held.
I know her nature: her spirits survive;
What this wine may do when her worth be
fed.
What flows into the heart of hers be heard,
And my shyness is still left to survive.
I lay these meadows as I took her calm,
But the satan was hired — a midnight sham.

Far to see my love Shine

"Thou" the beautiful queen, how shall I say?
Garlands run to thy feet; I ever bow.
Orchids of divine celebrate and grow;
The amazing times permit a heyday.
O! Winds so far enshine thy soul in trance;
Permit my haste and send me thy love thread.
The bard in me shall place — the words once said,
"O, blissful shrine as her welcoming dance,
Honey in pot and wild ways to the bee,
Which stings as much as my visage be gruff;
Over my brow another sting but laugh —
Heartfully I plead my soul at her glee."
O! My love is true and thy eyes be mine,
But thy eyes too far to see my love shine.

Waited all my Life

Why I reached her soon amidst the summer noon,
I could break the rules to cross her woe.
Across her dream — I sung the sweetest tune
That I could reach her heart what I still know.
Where could I find budding flowers of fame?
And why were her moods swayed to implode?
Where could I find her heart to love my shame?
And why was I waiting for her love abode?
The lasting memory — this morn would enshine
While my heart said, "how can my shine disown?"
This winter I missed — a love song with wine,
But my heart swung above and go with her crown.
But how could she go far away from me?
And why I waited my life so blindly!

Tragedy

No said her rug but continued his hug,
As his blood of passion searched for her bust.
While his twisted arms lifted her in smug,
He cheered her blushing chin, facing his lust.
He kissed her lips and pinched tip of her nose,
As he wriggled her tongue in a violent flow;
She held his arms so tight — a stylish pose
While danced her riddles to entrance his glow!
Reaching back home at her abode's wicket
She heard a voice, "run fast; cross the past!"
Fell at his wicket, her twisted thicket,
But still ran back home in the wild so vast!
A winter run that shrilled like a glitch:
She cried at a beach, his bestial ditch!

Elegy

Why I bought this candle — not like the Moon;
How could she allow me to touch her soon?
Why her pain visited her in a doom;
How could I find an eterinity soon?
I placed my fingers over its flame,
And touched her thirst for me, a step to prod.
Forbidden my busy tone, why this shame?
But my warmth — her love allowed it to brood.
And I loved her true like a tranquil shrine
That I brought her flowers, mastery shown!
I would be free or lead for her to shine,
But her lonesome tears would find her down.
Her heavy heart still waiting to find me;
A heart's broken cry in heavens to reach me!

With Glee

I'm the knight of a fanciful twilight
With ornaments like the sky and the stars:
By and why you sparkle like those stars — bright,
And my deepness in love waits for your dots.
Oceans apart but I never depart
When your love misses its turns as it frails;
My flow to the moon sings as I'm apart,
And poses like waves — dragging you in fears.
Chatters like the winds come close to your ears,
But missing in their tunes, crossing your fair;
Down in tears — I'm looking into your eyes,
But your whispers vanished far in the air.
By and then I cry as I see you flee,
But my thoughts are full; you fill them with glee.

Love & my Pebble strings

Like my Love living with the pebble springs,
So thee thy loving soul's mystical feast.
Hope and love strum at thy loving strings:
Written exquisite verses in a tryst!
Try, cry and dwell in times despite a fall
In a frequent toil, those fearless prevail.
Hail, shine in the bright of the Sun for a pal
While muted calm in a romantic sail.
Hurt while flirt — hesitant courting be mine,
O, amour aspired and its glee conspired!
In young, flying fresh love: stare, steer and dine;
Here in the ceasing times — romance transpired.
When I touch thy bust and raise a beast,
But thou rush to the priest for a bleak feast!

Enchanting Shine

My flowers sent a fascinating kiss,
But her bliss had left a scorching heat.
As the fire of my wings let yennings miss;
So far I stranded but her beautiful meet.
Guile as her calm, she disguised knots of charm
Where she had lived afar with a masked face.
Travelled by tram, she tried to reach her farm
When flares of fire had brushed her graceful days.
She swirled her hair while in a dusky fire:
A day at my scream at the stream of her dream.
Her masked face — had effaced winds of a mire;
That's a chance, she ran back to her lone whim.
But deep in my pine, her reverie to dine:
Her traces danced in the enchanting shine.

A solitary Dwell

Thy solitary dwell hey! The stars tell
Where my footsteps smell a cavern which
dwells:
"a cry" a low cry from thy chances hell
At the sands thou wander when the moonlight
dwells.
My soul stumbles at the entrance — alive;
A lonesome cave which dwells thy traces brave.
"strange" my heart heavy and sqeezed to survive,
A woody fen; thy spirit with this slave.
There upon the moon let my lady sit;
Her heart alone while crying more and more.
I come in the winds; thy sobs grow but print:
A blood of love which the wild winds forbear.
She wears her raiment is to set her free;
Her adorned jewels lost lustre and glee!

Love Deep

My worth is not grim to flow her in pair,
That's be her prowl, but I should lead my grit.
Her might so gushing to win her thirst;
Pity sowest troth — thunderous skies fear.
Where her sweetly uproar so wildly bear —
Her lips shuddering with a simple sigh.
When my heart muses in the vivid sky,
Grimness glimmers bright in the heartfelt fair.
Hides her bust in a fascinating cleave
She's in her outfit disrobs beauty's deal.
I felt her angel's kiss: warm I believe
Which my love dareth with all that sweat seal.
She closes our doors far behind to sleep
That my desperate love filling her deep!

Artistry Unknown

Artistry unknown but many fans I say;
She flew away in the air but I would wait!
Charm — my desire while she danced her day
And a day never came to know her straight.
She swang her moods in a mesmeric dance;
I watched her afar — my eyes ever found:
The grace which shone upon her like her ways
There I moved closer, her hair locks would bind!
O heart, thou tender that I slipped my dine,
But I drank my wine and recalled her half;
Amidst her dance she smiled to align —
Her strange posture in her rhythmic laugh.
How could I let her mesmeric trance flee?
And how could she stop her dance abruptly?

Lovely white Flowers

Lovely pure white flowers like pearls she picked,
Along the green grass of the trees for her hair.
Damsel by my side so brisk, I surprised
While she garnered flowers to bedeck her hair.
Her beauty so spright touched depths of my heart,
As she ran to cheer and walked along mine.
That those flowers in white at night might let
Chatters in the air and the fragrance enshrine!
She sang songs flowing depths of my bower
As thoughts arrested her iconic bond.
She is well in manner might mull over;
Why didn't I tell how beautiful her mind?
But why did she think what's other than me?
And how could she leave my stride so early?

Her Nakedness

Men ride or ravish his woman in play
While tarnishing her symbolic bliss to fret!
Her nature loomed to dread upon his way:
Her nakedness led; his pleasure was set.
He the beauty lover in his wild dreams,
But his dreams about a woman be kind.
And to thrive her prosperity to glimpse,
Wealth of distinct choices be remembered.
She is so beautiful in her rich attire
Like her skimpy frocks or long gowns with scarf.
Red lipstick or jewels give her fire;
Flowers like roses or jasmines engulf!
Why doff off attire or jewels to see —
Her nakedness in lavish lust to glee!

A thousand Flowers

When I consider thee as love I'm bent,
Thy frolicking plays shall take me so high.
That thy continence which thou abide by
Which my love binds O, thy soul God has sent.
My verve lives with thine love it's so pleasant;
Ever flowing spirit in lover's eye
Or love which may die but thy sentiment
Like to protect this strange love while thou cry!
Love life tremors whence loom upon my bed,
But such womanhood whence her truly gift!
Dreams which bear my wish her to wed but can't
In a princely flare, a thousand flowers paid
Won't last my lover's pride; oceans to rest:
So thy love life stands like waves at the best.

We meet Again

Strange — it's so much strange when we met again
When our laughters played in love so tender.
She had come behind mine edge closer to gain;
Her hair so lite wriggled fairly, wonder!
O heart! Pain until her fragrance melting
From those carved curves of love life in my fate;
My heart in her purest soul be lasting:
Wandering lures of her bond when I date.
O soul! I vanquished her foes in berserk,
And when she saw my soulful state of love,
But she turned back from mine — she lived to lurk.
The days fumed darker in the darkest show,
But how could she leave her darkness to me?
And how would I take so much grief bravely?

Woman of the Dark

He drives her dark but what will he embark?
Her blindness as the light she must be not known!
Deep within her heart, there's seed at the bark —
That's the dead bark but its no live roots known.
These roots deep like a mammoth O, her head!
The bed for her living whence she can grow.
The roots which fed the bark so much dead,
Killing her seed O, now her mind grows slow.
Who is the man to snare her in the stark?
But why can't her wild tumult be her boon?
How can she dare to bewitch snare to bare?
All whirls to swirl to lead her to the moon
Whence she grows and glows under the bark to free,
Her shackles of the man as she can be!

His soul be her Slave

Wait! He might bear or wear her awesome taste
No, her lavish splendour burden his night,
Watching for love, his heart broken in haste,
And like a growing dream he finds her might.
O, what next can test waters of this lake?
Filled in lure in her allure of its lores
In the dazzling sun — she basks her heart's stake
Of her mystic in the mountain dew woos.
Yet he still fasts till this date, his angel,
Mellow his love upon her fair lip s mist.
He feels for her dine — her soft corner dwell,
And for her love in his sweetness filled rest.
Still, he yens for her tender cheeks love wealth,
Be his divine — or his soul be her slave!

The Adultress

When I ponder how her bed plows a way,
It's a way ought to be incriminate.
Hard be the days charred her by people's fey
Whence her stigma wildly does perpetrate.
She leads in her rough but her life silence
While causing her distraught which may implode.
But she hides herself to shield from violence,
While her deep silence celebrates indeed.
There lives the lewd and his lewd thoughts may
glide;
She'll be so calm yet her tender fluff.
His brutal power couldn't penetrate,
As hell is the darkness that she may laugh.
O, how his mind be wrong to this lady,
And it's whose right to rant what to agree!

Nightly Woe

Like love life voyage, my life as her pair,
No, it doesn't wriggle but its beauty so fame.
Snow over a shack and her beauty hair
While a comely tender a lover's game.
For her beach and bath in a nature's shower,
Touring her score with her mystic in place;
Pretty or beauty name her much power
That I'm waned, if not her love line embrace.
Love like her frock lo! Those twirls of the dark,
So her blindly tweeted talk but words scream:
That care much all so fair, my beauty's talk
Amidst a simmering season's dream.
But all that she skirts is much my heart's low;
Her love sways away from my nightly woe.

A saddened Heart

Lustre! a diamond glitters of her eyes:
Deeper her stare into my calming mind,
When my quest asks thine to incite her pose,
Her curlish hair might strive a soulful bind.
But her heart has spoken what's plausible,
A love winter heart for the times much worth.
And to repose faith in mine at her will,
But the fire yet peace, be a morning mirth.
This reigning calm is my heartful aim;
A soulful wham into a lone tilled in life.
But no possible landscape by her tram,
And her soul can't drink nature in strife.
O, my saddened heart and brace her tight,
But unblossoming summer has ways tonight!

Change is no Love

When the new gown that she wears is no fun,
She's a different soul now but shouldn't.
Be the same but this damsel can not win
Whence she has changed her gown for his trust.
Roses her friends — deeply profuse fragrance,
But he chants to diffuse, that fragrance be changed
Wilted tone within her deep dolefulness
Or no beauty in her eyes she may be told.
He wishes to wed her but to tie,
But why does he ask her to change herself?
Those years such long she carries so dry
That a man dates or dotes when she herself;
Now a different soul — she should not be,
The name while calling it love what a plea!

Her dance my Trance

A day was no day when you were far away;
Pain at the bay, sunshine didn't abate.
Such was my shrine which should shine all the day;
Memory of your trace shouldn't fade fate.
Here weren't ways heart tried giving a chance;
All that went away from my love so spread.
Beyond the sky that your spell to entrance
When soul mine deep entered your world instead.
Many calls or texts while ready to cry
That I cried deep inside my heart but laugh.
I waited the day but couldn't find you try
To find me where I was; why you were tough.
But her suddenly dance my trance I see:
She swirls like a storm — my heart abruptly.

I can’t flee

O, pain of my heart — you go far away,
Don't wait and never wait while at my gate.
I cry that you fly far far in a way
But I shy in a sly, it's all my fate.
O, rain my train but you come at my face;
Now again I've shred my tears to wed
That you fall down but in my love in clouds;
How I go up if you fall down to spread:
Lies with no gain but all feign that I cry,
But rain takes my pain while ears turn deaf.
And still I trudge for your love that I vie,
That's all while my call to pain but I laugh.
But why do I still bear pain that I can't flee;
Why do I love her in my heart so deeply?

Silence of Love

Silence ever lits the candle in the night,
But amidst the brightness, life won't find!
A memory to swing while I'm to cling,
But her absence, a mighty thorn behind.
Fury and fight which real love may sow,
As always a selfless soul mine shall bow.
What I think may not be right to avow,
A word which spells my life she may allow.
O dare and how dare thine I shall not swear;
Who bears fire mine, I hide a secret flare?
She be my bliss but what if I miss her;
This life which belongs why can't I kiss her?
The pain in my heart is her soul I see,
But can her silence of love kill her for me?

Close to my Ways

My fetters — love spread whispers mute and lite
When I set her fun, love folks live hence long.
Dense in the tumultuous haze, spy her wing,
But she drops down straight to her knees so wait.
This time I wish, she would be to my right
That she be bosom friend for she can fling.
So soon to brush my sides, frisking in spring,
Nay, no wait for her, she's mine in bright!
Love me selfless and I love her but veiled:
Snow cover spreads the road but I reach fast.
To reach thee I am thine; no link be balked:
Swirling in my heart filled with her love last.
Words are love like birds why do fly always?
Think what I say, she be close to my ways.

Hearts Renew

I'm in my twenties that winter to stay;
Dinghy near lone waters — beauties aloft.
Her youth in knots but her body to sway,
Around her hips — her swing as she may hurt.
When I kiss her deep, that's all she breathes,
And her mountain like love; my roses bed.
My love sublime but she hides inner guise,
Which has mighty wings of love that I lead.
Shall I adore her amor fullest life?
It's her outfit's awesome cleave to watch though,
Love for decollete sparks but in her veil
In rain of the desert and waves much rough!
It's not a new love unlike her heart be,
And his heart renews what her love shall see.

Dwell in my Home

Love attitude that love be fair and just;
It's gratitude if her showers fill delight.
Of this milky way that the stars be bright
In their beatific glow if hearts not hurt.
Her soulful glee when it might be my bail —
But her flowery poses set ablaze:
Like an iris spread in an earnest craze,
My love shall dwell in her memories well.
Of those deep frozen eyes, my heart will weep,
But with the sweet river's flow, she shall swing.
Those songs embrace which I cry on to sing
Of her treasure, as my pleasure to dip.
And why her eyes filled livid till this day,
But why can't she dwell in my home each day?

Breathe her Life

Therefore, I bent my mind at her word play;
Her blazing eyes like a glow that I bet.
Her hair like a fire but no ire I say
What makes her truly mine, why can't I wait?
My tempest in her mind; she always cares,
But her heart has pain that she hasn't shared.
Pine, how she shines bright in my eye aligns;
Her sculpted figure when my eyeballs read.
That her worried dream, not a nightmare, why?
That my limitless love has made me tough.
O, she makes my life " a cry " that I lie,
And her tears on my chest while I laugh.
But why can't her hair brush my face closely?
And how will I breathe her life tenderly?

Due for Me

Her fair face touch has ignited incense
That her beauty defines is what I buy.
A lovely butterfly plays at the dale
When her slender figure is so intense.
I sip my wine for she closes her eyes,
And her love like flame that's what I can dwell.
Femininity grips love bud insides,
She's like a doll and her feet at the ball;
A great art of words — spreading firmament,
And beauty lonely this lady to bring;
Her own urges bud in a covenant
In a tender chuckle, her clutching wing:
Pretty her lips O, her hips shakingly
But the taste of her love buds due for me!

Flames

Flames of a brave girl shall instill her spine
From those conspiring men — inspire to kiss,
But she makes her grit stronger at ease
When she fills with flares, her sheen be a shrine.
She dotes until her date to love her fate,
And the titled queen holds this torch in faith.
She smells the footsteps until the brave path;
A guilt while men in their wild heart to sate!
Ye, artists of the world disdain her lane;
They seek Gods to draw her unholy blame.
While her unbent lines standing for the same,
Clouds erase these lines in a simple pain.
O! Why is the world whispers a wild cuss;
Why in the world her vespers - a mild crass?

The forsaken Child

I hear his whispers which his soul may sigh,
Let him speak to me O, what to bereave;
Face the wrath of the man — his life will die,
But his chants haven't brought me to believe:
Here in the woods while the evil has bread.
When the knife that gains blood in the game's
slain,
There shall live shame with other muted bleed;
How can warrant stigmatize just in vain?
The creep is the one, bewitching the corrupt;
There live times God sends to stifle his strife.
Love baits his saunter that flowers erupt;
Those bear the forsaken guise, a grave gaffe!
Let the moon binge or let the sun cringe,
But where can our aid leave a blissful binge?

Broken heart

My tide shall play love with darling in clay
Let thine a miracle that thou play brave.
Play with the sun; sea with life until day,
Thou wince and I astray but win shall save.
To tread thy dream, I climb a cliff of pangs;
My amor queen turns her glamour to wed.
Let me lit love, brace to wriggle in sins;
I tell tales to mould her loving clay bud.
This winter wild till spring times shall arrive;
My love derives, crossing the stars to sniff:
Thy touch and kiss serene, will thou not drive?
O, love of passion let her wings be tough.
In the toughest planes she paves my plea,
But how could her broken wings at the tree?

Crying Universe

Set my cause to thee, the grace of thy shine;
Let my soul to thee while grace is my low.
Bet my dreams for thee in grace of thy rain;
Let my freedom be in grace of her flow.
Where the world fears and the skies break
surprise,
The oceans lose waves: behold they may reek!
Here are the deeds bespeak pride which raise,
A prud's flourish but Angels may not speak!
Clouds depart to set apart in abrupt,
Taking away my breath; squeezing this life.
Of our harmony, just and peace in curt:
A blow to the world in her wilder rife!
Hark, oceans and thunders to go amiss
That all to wonder how to seek back peace!

Won't
Leave her

How I bear the dearth of thy bright shining,
But the pure sands heartfelt joy is singing.
When I'm still frozen — vigor is dying,
But various moods at best are moving.
The golden words which glitter are dating
While love and compassion are demanding.
I turn to her for thunderous dancing
While she captures my soul for arresting.
Ditties sing pretty her love embracing;
Heart of mine winning her love is flying.
I hear thy chatter, embrace; dating:
Pleasure is my dream, thou come in gliding.
If I ever sing, I will sing for her;
What I'm, how she knows but I won't leave her.

The Beast

If I praise her beauty, all she may say,
" I raise her to the skies, she fears fate. "
If I raise her passion, all she shall play:
O, she touches my cheeks to kiss my date.
Whether I run fear or tears to face,
She comes very nearly to the bed.
Whence she touches my lips — her tender brace;
I look upon her to kiss while I have told,
" This lady mine as my true love might vie. "
She looks into my eyes, a deep sense tough;
I take her by arms and embrace to die,
Which she loves to forget in her own ways
tough.
Ah! Here is the beast, which damns all at sea,
But I'm with an answer while set to free!

Master of the Paint

Lo, you may wink your eyes to flinch my dare;
Draweth a blossom affair " the unknown. "
My Angel who triggers a tragic fare
To my bosom friend's emphatic sojourn.
Honeybees stare at flowers to compare
When this summer time winds searching
her farm.
I'm in a prison while drowning in there,
And this hilly town is a full grown sham.
Lo, my Angelina that my heart's raise:
Why are you so warm? Aren't you my charm?
My song able, a melodious reprise;
A soft pain to drain: dying way to qualm!
Your soft hair coils in the sweet-mood-wed,
Like a master of paint, your lavish spread.

Need Neither

She and her loneliness have stopped today;
Yes, if I've scaled in my early date.
We have wriggled in love on a heyday,
And flown to the west to find the sunset!
Rainbow over symphs has poised our days
In growing thickets spring a nearly cloud,
Poses or roses, and sparkling love ways
For our love shines into the dawn, we tried.
But the eyes of the night can see to lie,
The evil bedevils and veils ways rough,
That at times, that her unpleasant tie
We no longer feel ourselves while laugh.
Aloof widely, how long we can be
All the poor glimpses, we well mean to be!

ELICITATION

SONNETS
1 - 30

PHILIP ISUKAPATI

SONNET -1

"you" poet can think about entire universe and depict it in your words. You think about us; your wit effaces our tearful world. But we wonder, how our thoughts flow to you?

SONNET -2

Mother Earth! There is no balm which can cure wounds we caused. But I never hurt you! I promise God that I'm his call while from my help nature can avoid hurt, so let me propagate the same that the Earth in me; when I do it, my mind is fruitful and bloom my mother Earth!

SONNET -3

I wanna love a woman: just like or war like; also wanna know what makes me drive a woman? That I wake up in her surprise, but she hates my love for her. Then, why should I love her like an unwise? It is easy to love but it is more difficult to like someone, since love stems from generosity while like is for a particular quality.

SONNET -4

Ants and their colony lost their homes, and they keep searching by wandering through cities known. Even when they searched interior hamlets for their homes, they couldn't find any, as their mud has been vanished as human homes.

SONNET -5

It's witty! If you say that I'm your money then, I may ask you to sleep with me. But if you say I'm your honey then, I'll ask, why do you need money — knowing that I'm your honey, we date each other while I wonder how money is your love! On contrary, you can love me in sans money!

SONNET -6

Pearl! A ghost like sand driven you to create a balm from that crushing pain; you finally died. Your remarkable shadow that's after death, created a moonlike spark: titled "Pearl" a true love!

SONNET - 7

Trees in plenty yield: life, fruit, shelter and breath. We can't test whether the Moon has trees while stars can bring air. But why do we cut them just like that, for our pleasure! How and when we cut a tree, unknowingly — we are taking revenge on our own selves!

SONNET -8

He is addicted to her but her bitterness for him while his warlike self freed her since his mot. Her fame raised a million claps as her soul still dumped his past but his respectable character stinged her to brew his love; now she's waiting for his heart warming games.

SONNET -9

Jail! A punishment by incarceration but what if we jail our mind, body and soul! Hey, it can blossom a real freedom of thought. A physical confinement mostly can also confine our minds productively in turn, growing us in our thoughts. But why do we call it a punishment? And why can't we call it a happy moment?

SONNET -10

She met a guy while she held him tight. But he deserted her! She pleaded him but couldn't get him back while he told her lies. She was left alone and sank in his selfishness that she bore her pain while fate didn't leave her. Nine months later, she's very happy about the baby which she delivered instead! Kudos to femininity!

SONNET -11

Prince, a friend of all pretty girls but cautious while moving with them. They wait for his love but he mutes his tone while a slender beauty captures his gaze and dances around him to surround him! Like a sylph — she smiles and laughs at him, but he choses the one with no joy to free!

SONNET -12

Your fragrance pervades all around mine that I have become your bait. I'm waiting for you here that I won't miss your fragrance. When I walk, your memories race; I'll be busy still, waiting for you to pair with me. But all this has become a poison for me!

SONNET - 13

Compared my love with a love letter and its carrier — dove. The carrier of love is passive and an eagle grips the dove while her feathers torn away as she cries. My trials are cringing but seeking divine to inspire my love. Falling from above while I know my love lives all the above — skies!

SONNET -14

My love so blind! I send roses, I gift jewels; there you come! Your aura keeps growing along my footsteps! You wear jasmine while pose; I come so near but you close. I glance and I wait but you shut door in my silent fate!

SONNET -15

You whirl me, petrify me and poison my mind but my heart never receded; my love never diminished. Finally, you say — your love is sky; why I'm late!

SONNET -16

Can rain feign what should belong to me? You deflected my love but I'm skillful enough to fight while can't hide my love from you. Even when you don't favor my love, how can I take away my shine from you?

SONNET -17

I can't take away my eyes from you; I depict your beauty in plenty. I've become weak just for you, but I can't fly to reach you as you have gone far away. And it's all your pretense, so I fall so low out of love!

SONNET -18

Crazy moments! Many wait for her while marriage. I'm with her but she's unsure. I go back home for peace but still dream her. Thereafter, We meet at the downhill and come to an understanding. But finally, my tears grace the occasion.

SONNET - 19

You are my zeal, you stifle my sadness and make me come out of my fear. A little away from you that I run into tears, but when you are close, you heal me like a wand! But you've captured my soul while disappeared in space as I'm trying to know: your whereabouts!

SONNET - 20

If I dislike why I should bear her while others are glad. She's is like a warrior, even men can't lure her and even witches dread at her! How could she be like this? I chant some other's name, asking myself to lit a new affair. I'm with a lot of turbulence but now all conventions confine.

SONNET -21

She is flying: wants to be lonely; I'm sad as she has left me for her fear. Amidst my dry days, she shines; somewhere, she tells me to choose her fear and when I do it, whatever is the separation "no longer there!"

SONNET -22

"her" his past love died in his bad fate! Angelina has come for his purity, skill and awareness but she's shy and coys away. And now she has become his joy, cloy or ploy; unless she accepts kisses his — she evades!

SONNET -23

When I fly for you, I fall to the ground and broke my wings. Hey! I run on the ground to the streams, where I get peace. Hereafter, like Pegasus I fly back to the skies; I hear you from far away but I fly to the freedom of my heart!

SONNET -24

Love life: full of dolefulness and melancholy while fun only till bed. But he enjoys all mourn with her and ready to face life challenging thorns yet forget his troubles while live beyond their bed!

SONNET - 25

Thou (God) created me for your having freedom but where is my freedom? This is the question of a hungry child, a hungry man or a hungry woman. All bright but the other side dark; even if they cry — none to care, and I think that holy power alone may dare to help them!

SONNET - 26

The nature is so beautiful, but the world is ready to deprive of its beauty since, we prefer constructing buildings to protecting nature; hence, her fret! In this fast growing world, nature's beauty has become short-lived, so I care to see her growing.

SONNET - 27

When my souls seeks God, I cry; what I seek from God, the world has deprived me. Still, I speak to God to try; if he supports, spirits alive. The world filled in bloodshed since the world full of arms but why do we need arms except for our suffering or death?

SONNET -28

Nature filled her beauty there I stared at her; trying to prove myself and when I asked her to be my side, I even knew she was arrogant. But she's in her nuptial moods while I was sad at her. Asking myself will she ever hear me: O her honored paradise!

SONNET -29

She was a pure heart; gifted him honey like love. In her life time, he experienced many a shade of her love: her embrace, emotion, win over talk, pranks; admiration for all the cheer he embodies. Now, he looks at the heavenly grace but neither her voice nor her face — can he hear nor face!

SONNET -30

Always touch her cheeks to start my day as she smiles opening her eyes. But suddenly she forgets her past; her memory fades away. I ask, why does she forget me and how she disgrace her own faith in me?